Milet Publishing
Smallfields Cottage, Cox Green
Rudgwick, Horsham, West Sussex
RH12 3DE England
info@milet.com
www.milet.com
www.milet.co.uk

First English–Chinese edition published by Milet Publishing in 2013

Copyright © Milet Publishing, 2013

ISBN 978 1 84059 822 3

Original Turkish text written by Erdem Seçmen
Translated to English by Alvin Parmar and adapted by Milet

Illustrated by Chris Dittopoulos
Designed by Christangelos Seferiadis

Printed and bound in Turkey by Ertem Matbaası

My Bilingual Book

Taste

尝

English–Chinese

Milet

Close your eyes, taste this drink . . .

闭上双眼，品尝饮品滋味。。。

Water or soda, what do you think?

清水抑或是苏打水，你喝的是什么呢？

How do you know which one it is?

你如何知晓自己喝到的是什么？

Do your mouth and tongue feel a fizz?

你的口中和舌尖是否感觉到一阵兴奋?

Your mouth and tongue let you taste drinks and food.

口齿舌尖告诉你饮用的饮料和品尝的食物。

They tell you what tastes bad and what tastes good!

它们告诉你口中的滋味几何！

Your taste senses bitter, sour, sweet,

在吃饼干时，味觉

and salty, like the crackers you eat.

带给你苦涩甘咸的多样体验。

Some like the taste of chocolate best.

有如巧克力般的美妙滋味。

Most like the taste of medicine less!

亦有如良药般苦口难咽!

It's fun to think about yummy sweets,

美味的糖果总是乐趣无穷，

but eating too many is bad for your teeth!

但过多的甜食也会对牙齿造成伤害！

Foods like peppers can be so hot!

辛辣食品会异常热辣！

Your taste will tell you to eat them or not.

味觉会告诉你是否适合食用。

Some tastes go together and some really don't mix,

一些味道会相互融合，而另外一些则总是各行其道，

like that banana and cheese sandwich you are about to fix!

正如你难以抗拒的香蕉奶酪三明治！

These delicious fruits deserve a nibble.

美味的水果让人不容错过。

They're good for your body and irresistible!

有益身体健康，同时也是令人无法抗拒的美味。

Trying different foods makes your taste sense grow.

尝试不同的食物，延伸你的味觉。

Your world gets bigger, the more foods that you know!

随着对世界认知的扩展，你会拥有更多的各种味蕾体验。